Seasons of Life

By Denise LaLande

"To everything, there is a season, and a time to every purpose under heaven." Ecclesiastics 3:1

*To my grandchildren and great-grandchildren.
May this book of devotions help navigate you through
the seasons of life.*

My Diagnosis

It was in 1995 when my husband, Dean, and I moved to Georgia from Michigan. About a year later, I noticed I was having trouble with my speech. As time went on, my ability to speak gradually got worse. For the first five years, I went from doctor to doctor, looking for an answer. No one knew what was wrong. I decided at that time to go to a speech therapist, thinking that she could help me. She was the first doctor to point out that she thought it was a neurological problem and suggested that I see a neurologist.

One day in 2001, I heard of a disorder called Dystonia, which can affect your speech. I made an appointment with a neurologist specializing in this disorder at the Emory Neurology Clinic. After examining me, the doctor ruled out Dystonia. However, the doctor said he would like another neurologist to examine me. He thought that I might have ALS but did not mention it to me. The neurologist specialized in ALS, Amyotrophic Lateral Sclerosis, also known as Lou Gehrig's disease. After the doctor examined me, he said he wanted to look over his notes and then get back to me in fifteen minutes. Fifteen minutes later, I was sitting across from him. My son-in-law was with me.

The doctor said he had good news and bad. Which one did I want to hear first? I told him the good news. He asked me if I had ever heard of ALS, and I told him I had. I could feel a chill go through me. The good news was that I didn't have ALS but a disease called Primary Lateral Sclerosis, an ALS variation. PLS is a rare neuromuscular disease characterized by progressive muscle weakness in the voluntary muscles, and I was also told there was no cure. I learned later that there were only 1,500 patients in this country with PLS.

When my son-in-law and I returned to the car, it began to sink in, and I thought, "I couldn't live like this." I wasn't expecting this kind of diagnosis, and neither was my family. My husband and children were working, and my son-in-law was available to take me. I was glad he was there, but the diagnosis was surprising for both of us. The truth was I didn't want to live like that! I quickly dismissed that thought and began to think of God and His Word. God's promises of never leaving or forsaking me began to flood my heart. By the time I got home, I was at peace with God and my disease. I knew nothing could touch me without His divine permission! He had a reason for it.

Several years after my diagnosis, most of my ability to converse was gone due to tongue weakness from nerve damage. The disease was also affecting my legs. I noticed my hands were moving at a slower pace as well. I often felt on the outside looking in at church, set apart from others. Communication is vital to our lives!

I knew I had to do something about this to bring communication back into my life. I decided I would bring a notepad with me to church. I couldn't write fast, but at least I was communicating again! It made a difference in my life. A year later, I was introduced to a small computer called a Dynawrite. This could enable me to communicate more swiftly with others!

God was meeting my needs in so many ways! It's not to say that I didn't have my moments because I did, but God's Word always wins over me, and He is still working in my life. There is a saying, "Please be patient. God is not finished with me yet." Well, that's me! I have learned that my trial is no greater than anyone else's. God's grace is sufficient no matter what we are going through. His grace balances out every trial. "But my God shall supply all your needs according to His riches in glory by Christ Jesus." Philippians 4:19

If we could look into the future to see what lies ahead for us, we would fret and worry, anticipating its arrival! These things are hidden in the sovereignty of God. Each day has enough trouble of its own. Setting goals for the future is good, but worrying about what tomorrow may hold is fruitless! For each day, God's grace will be sufficient! "Take therefore no thought for the morrow: for the morrow shall take thought for the things of itself. Sufficient unto the day is the evil thereof." Matthew 6:34

In 2001, the idea came to me to write memories of my childhood for my granddaughters. I decided to put them into poems. When I went to bed at night, the thoughts began rolling in. I had a great time writing my memories! There were times of laughter as I remembered the shenanigans my brothers and I got into! Then, I started to write short stories about my Christian experiences that left an impression on my life. It expanded to fiction and then to devotionals. God was allowing me to express myself through writing. It was a great outlet for me. He was still meeting my needs!

There are times when we will feel alone in our trials. Spiritually, we must be moving forward, for without a goal or vision in our lives, we become stagnant, losing sight of who we are in Christ Jesus. We begin to turn inward, seeing ourselves as useless and not worth much. We must turn outward to God and His Word, not inward, and claim all He has for us! Having a disability and becoming more restricted compounds this all the more! At these times, we must pray to God, asking for His help in restoring the vision of what He has planned for our lives and reaching for the goal He has set before us.

We all get discouraged at times, feeling we should be doing more. This is where our faith comes in. We seek the face of God, trusting that He will lead us on the path He has ordained for us. "He giveth power to the faint; and to them that have no might he increaseth strength. Even the youths shall faint and be weary, and the young men shall utterly fall; but they that wait upon the Lord shall renew their strength; they shall mount up with wings as eagles; they shall run, and not be weary; and they shall walk, and not faint." Isaiah 40:31

Let us trust God with our lives, knowing what is stated in His Word. "Being confident of this very thing, that He which hath begun a good work in you will perform it unto the day of Jesus Christ." Philippians 1:6

We may have no control over the trials that God allows to come our way, but we can live each day serving our Savior, the Lord Jesus Christ, with the abilities He has given us!

Seasons

"To everything, there is a season, and a time to every purpose under heaven." Ecclesiastics 3:1. When we go through life, we experience different seasons when God allows different trials to come our way. Their duration may be short, long, and even to the end of life, serving God's purpose. Friendships come and go, as do hardships and all trials of life. Our seasons can have a negative or positive effect on us. Do we trust God when we go through different seasons, or do we go against them? Have you ever fought a fierce wind blowing against you and found yourself getting nowhere? This is what it's like when we fight against God's will. If we persevere in our strength, we can resist His will and think that we can change our season, but we find ourselves getting nowhere.

We will all be affected differently according to God's plan as He brings about His purpose in our lives. Like our seasonal weather, changes can come quickly, sometimes without warning. Our lives can change quickly, too. When we find ourselves in the midst of a storm, the winds of a trial bearing down on us, there is only one person who can calm the storm: God Himself. "He maketh the storm a calm, so that the waves thereof are still." Psalm 107:29

We will all face storms that cause us to reel and our faith to waver. God's sustaining grace will see us through the storm. When we feel like a storm is overtaking us, remember God's everlasting arms that will hold us up and calm the storm. "Which holdeth our soul in life, and suffereth not our feet to be moved." Psalm 66:9

When a storm is over, the sun surrounds us with warmth and light. God is our shield in times of trouble. When the storm is passing through, He surrounds us with His love. "For the Lord God is a sun and shield: no good thing will he withhold from them that walk uprightly." Psalm 84:11

We have heard this saying, "April showers bring May flowers." Can we think of flowers as God's blessings? When we have gone through a difficult trial or a season in our lives, God gives us a blessing many times afterward. "And I will make with them and the places around my hill a blessing; and I will cause the shower to come down in his season; there shall be showers of blessings." Ezekiel 34:26

Our seasons should cause spiritual growth and draw us closer to the Lord. Will you trust Him? He knows our seasons and has a purpose for them.

Resilient

While watching T.V., I heard the word resilient mentioned in a conversation. For some reason, it stood out for me, and I was intrigued by it. I thought it would be good to write about it, but then I dismissed it. During the week, I heard this word mentioned three more times and decided this was a powerful word to write about. You could preach a sermon around it–the Christian life, trials, and suffering!

Before I got carried away with this word, I would look it up in the dictionary. Even though I knew the meaning, I wanted to get the full impact of it. Resilient–Bouncing or springing back into shape, position, elastic, recovering strength, spirits, good humor, quickly: buoyant. Now, doesn't that sound like the Christian life?

Bouncing or springing back into shape–we all, as Christians, get discouraged and downhearted. Somewhere along the way, God has a way of getting our attention through a sermon, as we read the Bible, or hearing someone's testimony which encourages us to get back into the Christian race. Some spring back slowly, others get into shape quickly. A lot depends on our attitude and willingness to trust God when the going gets tough. Sometimes, we forget our position in Jesus Christ and what His death on the cross has done for us. Not only does the cross bring salvation to those who repent of their sins, receiving Jesus Christ as their personal Savior, but we are now in a new position to claim all that God has given us in His Word!

We find recovery strength through His promises, a lifting of our spirit, and finding once again the joy of the presence of God. Our good humor comes back as we rejoice in the Lord. The joy of the Lord is our strength! Being buoyant, we can rise above our circumstances, quickly regaining ground we lost as we refocus on the Word of God.

Yes, resilient is a powerful word. It tells us what the Christian life is about. With God's help from the Holy Spirit, we can be resilient in our Christian walk.

A Challenge

Years ago, my granddaughter, Jessica, and I went to the outdoor mall in the summertime. While shopping, we decided to stop and have lunch and went into a restaurant to eat. While sitting eating, Jessica said, "Grandma, I have a question to ask you." She had a firm look when I asked her, "What did she want to know?" Jessica was a teacher in an elementary school, and suddenly, I felt like a student and had no idea what she would ask me, making me slightly nervous. With a serious look, she wanted to know why I kept my devotions and stories locked up on my computer. Feeling relieved, I thought about her question, answered what I thought was a logical answer, and said, "I was saving them for my grandchildren and any great-grandchildren and even great-great-grandchildren. I wanted them to know me. It was like leaving a part of me behind." That answer did not satisfy her, and she said I should share it with others who may need to read your devotions. To make a long story short…she won the debate! She cornered me and left me no way out! Her gift from God was definitely an "exhorter"!

God used Jessica to motivate me because I lacked the confidence to share my devotions. The Lord knew this was hidden in me, and He sent someone to help me, to reason through why I should share my writings with others. It was not for my edification but for God's glory! Jessica was the right person for God to use. She was straightforward and firm and would not settle for me to talk my way out but yet had a gentle spirit about her.

Was shopping at the mall God's timing? I think it was! He was going to use Jessica to motivate her grandma! I'm glad He did, for I have enjoyed sharing with others and encouraging them through my writings.

God's timing is always perfect. Nothing is out of His control! Find out what your spiritual gift is in the Bible. All Christians have at least one gift, and others have many. Then, use your gift for edifying others to the glory of our Lord Jesus Christ!

The Choir

It was Christmas Eve when Dean and I decided to go and visit his sister, Wilma, and her husband, Bob. They lived about twenty minutes away from us. It was dusk outside as we left our home. The snow was falling, causing a picture postcard Christmas Eve. After we arrived at their home, they invited us to come and eat dinner with them. After we ate, Wilma and I decided to go to church that evening.

The church that Dean and I attended canceled services that night because of a prediction of heavy snowfall. Wilma mentioned there was a little white church down the road from her that she had thought about visiting. Dean and Bob decided they didn't want to go out and suggested we stay in because of the snow. They had already settled down with their coffee and were enjoying the warmth of the home.

We decided to go since it was just near their home. We wanted to see if they had services that night. Wilma and I arrived at the church and saw they had services. As we walked in the front door, people immediately began to shake our hands in greeting, giving us a warm welcome! The service was about to start, so we found a couple of seats. Looking around, I estimated there were about twenty people there. We were told the children were in another church area having their Christmas program and party.

The choir director approached the pulpit and asked the choir to come up to the loft. As I watched the choir make their way to the front, I was impressed to see how large their choir was until I looked around the sanctuary and realized Wilma and I were the only two people left sitting in a pew! Everyone else had left their seats and gone up into the choir loft! We looked at each other in amazement. Were they going to sing for just two people? We felt awkward sitting there, knowing we were the only two people sitting in the sanctuary.

They didn't know us, and we didn't know them. Sensing our discomfort, the choir director leaned over the pulpit peering down at us, and said, "Well, the two of you might as well come up here, too." Wilma looked at me and said, "What do you think? Should we go up?" I said we might as well, as everyone else was up there. So on Christmas Eve night, we joined the church choir. That choir didn't hold back! They lifted their voices unto the Lord! Before we knew it, we were enjoying it right along with them. They sang one Christmas carol after another, and I could hear the sopranos, tenors, and basses singing their parts. It was wonderful! Then we were dismissed to go down to the sanctuary. As we took our seats, we were surprised that the choir director was also the pastor! We continued to be blessed as he brought forth his message.

With the service over, people again shook our hands and thanked us for joining them in their choir. They were glad we came and invited us to come back again. On the way home, we decided that if all churches could be like this, it would make a difference in the world! When we think back to our choir experience, it brings a smile and laughter to our hearts! It was a once-in-a-lifetime experience I'm sure we will never experience again. As I reflected back to that Christmas Eve night, I thought of the blessings Wilma and I would have missed if we had not gone to the little white church down the road.

Rest

After entering my fifteenth year with Primary Lateral Sclerosis, I asked myself, "What have I learned throughout these years about God and myself?"

I belong to a PLS group on the Internet. One of our PLS patients wrote online, "After having PLS for eleven years or more, she finds herself really struggling more and more with this disease. She needed help!" I pondered her words and wondered how I handled living with PLS. I admit I had many unrestful moments during my first five years with PLS. Before my diagnosis, my speech was getting worse as time passed, and I would experience anxiety, not knowing what was wrong with me. I knew that something was wrong, but I couldn't find a doctor who could give me an answer. I even sometimes wondered if it was all in my mind and that I was causing my speech problem.

Finally, after five years of searching, I had a name for my speech problem. My diagnosis was Primary Lateral Sclerosis. It was a weight lifted off my shoulders to have a name for my condition. On the way home from the ALS Clinic, I trusted God with my disease and have felt His comfort over the years.

Many times, down through the years, I have told God I expected great things from Him! I knew that He would back up His Word. I didn't know what great things I was expecting, only that I had great expectations. God knew what I needed! Among the great things He gave me was a deeper knowledge of His eternal love. His thoughts were continually on me, and He is sovereign over everything, even my circumstances. I realized that by having PLS, God would take me to a much deeper level of understanding His role in my life. He would demonstrate the blessings He has prepared for me and teach me how to "rest" in Him. As I read the PLS group's posts online, I soon realized that each of us would go at his own pace with this disease. Some of us would progress very slowly, while others would progress rapidly. We couldn't use how long we had PLS to compare our progression with one another. I was learning to rest in The Lord.

When I was first diagnosed, I was told to lead a stress-free life and that I shouldn't do something if I didn't want to do it! Stress would cause my disease to progress faster. I really had to think that one over! In our day and age, how does one avoid stress? The answer was to learn to "rest" in the Lord. The last thing I needed to do was to go into battle with my disease! I needed to trust God and not dwell on my limitations as my disease progressed. I had trials before my PLS and knew that trials waited ahead of me, too. Faith and trust would have to be my companions as I travel through this life and learn to "rest" in the Lord.

"Thou wilt keep him in perfect peace, whose mind is stayed upon thee: because he trusteth in thee." Isaiah 26:3

Crossing Bridges

I remember my mother saying to me as a teenager, "Don't cross your bridges before you get to them!" In my heart, I knew what she meant. I was a worrier! I wanted to know before anything happened what was ahead of me. All of us will find ourselves facing a bridge that God brings into our lives. We find ourselves standing at the foot of a bridge, debating whether to cross it or not. Do we step onto it thinking we can handle what may be waiting for us on the other side? Pride has a way of deceiving us, giving us the wrong kind of confidence. When we take that first step, the next step is a little easier to take. Eventually, we become confident that we can take care of whatever is on the other side! As we venture out and get closer to the other side of the bridge, we are shocked to see what is waiting for us! We soon realize it was more than we could bear alone, and knowing where, when, and why is suddenly no longer necessary. We needed help all along. We turn around and start crossing back to where we first started. We see a figure standing at the foot of the bridge, and as you get closer, you soon realize it is The Lord Jesus Christ! Now you run to Him, His arms outstretched, waiting for you to return. "For I the Lord God will hold thy right hand, saying unto thee; fear not; I will help thee." Isaiah 41:13

Only God can safely take us over our bridges in life. He knows the strength of them and what they can endure. He is the one who constructs them. He may hold our hand as we cross, or lift us into His loving arms, carrying us safely. He is the only one who knows what is on the other side. Some Christians are unaware of the bridges before them; they have learned to walk by faith by trusting God. They had crossed bridges before and learned that when a trial comes their way, they must put their complete trust in Jesus Christ to guide them on their journey. Our bridges in life will not all be the same in length. Some will be longer than others, and some shorter. Each bridge constructed by God is to bring about His purpose in our lives.

Christians, don't cross your bridges before you get to them! Instead, trust God to guide you and bring us safely to the other side. Reaching the other side with Jesus Christ, we find that our faith and trust in Him have been strengthened. "I will instruct thee and teach thee in the way which thou shall go: I will guide thee with mine eye." Psalm 32:8

A Home

Have you ever watched a home being built? If it is built of bricks, you will need a bricklayer; if it is built of wood, you will need a carpenter. It's fascinating to watch it rise up into a beautiful home. But before you start, you will need a designer who can create a design to fit your needs. Have you ever thought of yourself as being a home? God calls your body a temple. 1 Corinthians 6:19 "What? Know ye not that your body is the temple of the Holy Ghost which is in you, which ye have of God, and ye are not your own?" In our earthly home made of brick and wood, we maintain it with painting, plumbing, and electrical repairs, fixing a leaking roof, and even spraying for bugs! We do this to maintain its value. We also decorate the inside of our home, giving it a comfortable atmosphere. Our home should represent a touch of Heaven; as we enter, it should be a refuge from the outside world.

What about our body that God calls a temple that houses His Holy Spirit? I must admit that we paint it at times and have plumbing and electrical problems, and of course, we spray it for different purposes as we try to maintain its outward appearance.

Have you ever gone into a home with the outside looking great, but after going inside, you find it in an awful mess? We can do all kinds of things to the outside of our bodies to give them a good appearance, but on the inside, it can be a mess!

God is not concerned about a little paint or anything that enhances our outward body as long as it's done in moderation. As Christians, we represent God! How we maintain the inside of ourselves determines how God's light will be reflected outwardly. If we live with unconfessed sin, we quench the Holy Spirit and His working through us. "Quench not the Spirit." 1 Thessalonians 5:19

Just as we clean and maintain our earthly homes, God also wants us to keep our heart clean. "Create in me a clean heart, O God; and renew a right spirit within me." Psalm 51:10

A messed-up life does not glorify the Lord. We use different tools to clean the inside of our earthly homes–vacuums, dusters, soap, etc. God has also given us a tool to help clean up our inside, His Word! "Thy word have I hid in mine heart, that I might not sin against thee." Psalm 119:11

To enter our homes, we unlock the door with a key. We also hold the key to our heart that allows Jesus Christ to come in. "Behold, I stand at the door, and knock; if any man hear my voice, and open the door, I will come in to him, and will sup with him, and he with me." Revelation 3:20

Our faith in the Lord Jesus Christ is the key that unlocks the door to our hearts and invites Him in. Let us clean our temple by sweeping out sin through confession and walking according to His Word so that the light of Jesus Christ shines. "Blessed is the people that know the joyful sound: they shall walk, O Lord, in the light of thy countenance." Psalm 89:15

A Love Letter

He told me that I was the apple of his eye and that He would love me forever! He said He would always care for me and never let me down. If I had a need to come to Him, He would take care of it. He also said that He would help me find direction in life, and if I stumbled, He would pick me up.

You might ask, "Who said this to you?" Was it someone who was a lover of my soul, a close friend, a brother, or even a father? He is all of that and more!

You might say, "Where is this love letter that I may read for myself?" (It was sent to me thousands of years ago, but I didn't receive it until 1966.)

You might wonder, "Could I receive this love letter for myself?" Yes! In fact, He sent it to everyone in the world! All you must do is receive it and believe it is true in your heart.

You might know, "He died for your sins, that you can have eternal life and live with Him forever!"

You might ask, "Who is this person?" He is the Lord Jesus Christ, and His love letter is His Word, The Holy Bible! "For God so loved the world that He gave His only begotten son. That whosoever believeth Him, should not perish but have everlasting life." John 3:16

A Mission

I have heard people say that their mission is to be an environmentalist, humanitarian, one who saves animals, and the list goes on and on. Their goal is to create interest and bring about change. A mission has a cause and effect behind it. Having a mission in life creates a desire to achieve a goal by bringing recognition to a cause. Many try to get recognition for a cause through support from other people, the media, or foundations.

Because we live in a land of democracy, we have the freedom to have our voices heard, which can be persuasive. This is why we need to keep everything in perspective. We live in a society where logic has taken a back seat, and rationality and the ability to reason sit alongside it!

In our world, we see people trying to eradicate God's voice from society. By doing this, they can move in with their own agenda of "no accountability." They don't want to hear that their life of wrongdoing is called sin. As we draw nearer to the second coming of Christ, the world's voice gets louder, hoping to drown out the voice of God. Although men would like to squelch His voice by restricting where it can be heard, God's message will always continue. The Pharisees tried to stop the voice of Jesus Christ by hanging Him on the cross. They thought this would end His mission.

There wasn't a voice loud enough or powerful enough that could stop Him!

So, where does that leave us Christians? Have our voices become quiet? I must say "no" because God still rules the universe. Nothing is out of His control; His timetable for mankind has never been thwarted. Missionaries still go to the mission field here and abroad, proclaiming the Gospel that Jesus Christ saves. Their mission is to have a cause and effect on those who receive God's message. What is your mission in life, and what should it be? Our cause is to be committed to Christ, and the effect will bring about change in our lives and the world.

A Purpose

I was listening to a Christian speaker on TV and heard this statement, "Without a purpose in life, we can lose hope." I thought about myself. What purpose did I have? I felt heaviness in my spirit. Having Primary Lateral Sclerosis and being very limited in what I could do physically, what purpose did I have? My mind went to those who had capabilities that I didn't have. My voluntary muscles weaken from this disease year by year, making it difficult to interact with people. I found myself focusing on my limitations. I could no longer maintain a conversation with others or move about as I once did, yet I have always had hope as a Christian. If I haven't lost hope in God and in life, why then did I feel that I didn't have a purpose?

Something was missing in my judgment. The speaker had caught me off guard! How quickly Satan can derail us in our thoughts! 2 Corinthians 2:11 "Lest Satan should get an advantage of us: for we are not ignorant of his devices." When we let our defenses down, not depending on the Word of God, even the smallest doubt allows Satan to tempt us. What was my purpose?

Then God spoke to my heart, saying, "I did have a purpose, which was to glorify Him." I knew this because, upon my commitment to Christ, this had been my request, and for a few moments, I had lost my perspective. I consider it an honor and a privilege to glorify the Lord. Each day that goes by, when I think of my purpose in life, I rejoice in the knowledge that whatever limitations we have, our purpose is to glorify God with what we have been given! "For ye are bought with a price: therefore glorify God in your body and spirit, which are God's." 1 Corinthians 6:20. To have a purpose is to have hope!

"Happy is he that hath the God of Jacob for his help, whose hope is in the Lord his God." Psalm 146:5

A Slippery Slope

My slippery slope is my attitude that I have to keep in check. We may not be able to control our circumstances, but we can certainly control our attitude toward them. Self-pity or wrong attitudes cannot be part of a Christian's life because it will take us one step closer toward a slippery slope. Once we step out onto it, it's hard to break the momentum from sliding down. This is why Jesus Christ tells us to check our attitude toward ourselves, others, and God.

Based on the principles in His Word, negative thinking can play no part in a Christian's life. "Why me," cannot be part of our thinking. When we feel ourselves slipping, and there will be days when we feel like we are, we must stay focused on God's promises. Psalm 37:24 says, "The law of his God is in his heart; none of his steps shall slide." I think God receives no greater pleasure than to have us fully trust Him. He has promised us in His Word that He has a strong arm, and His promises are sure. "Though he fall, he shall not be utterly cast down: for the Lord upholdeth him with his hand." Psalms 37:24

As children, many of us have stood on something high and had our father hold out his arms, saying, "jump!" and laughing, we leap into his arms, trusting he will catch us. Our Heavenly Father wants us to have child-like faith, trusting that He will uphold us and keep us from a slippery slope. "When I said my foot slippeth; thy mercy, O Lord, held me up." Psalm 94:18

A Song

Back in the seventies in Michigan, a group of us ladies from my church were going to a Women's Retreat in Canada. The retreat was held in a beautiful auditorium that had three balconies and could hold one thousand people. Before the guest speaker came to the podium, an announcement was made regarding a special singer who had come to present a musical selection. The announcer gave a background with her attributes. I was impressed with her credentials. After they announced her name, an elegant lady came to the podium. I wondered as I watched her what type of song she would sing. Would she choose a classical song demonstrating her singing abilities or an older hymn complimenting her voice? We had been told that she was a Contralto.

We waited in anticipation; then, she began singing without musical accompaniment. I think we were all surprised by the song that she chose. By this time, I'm sure you are asking, "What song did she sing?" She sang "Jesus Loves Me," a simple, childlike song in a slowed-down tempo and with deep emotion. When the singer had completed her song, there was quietness throughout the auditorium. Our hearts were stirred as she sang from her heart and ministered to our spirit. Leaving us with no doubt that Jesus loved us! Sometimes, we think bigger is better, but sometimes, a little is just enough.

A Winter's Night

In Michigan, a winter storm could come on quickly! On a Tuesday evening, I decided to go to our church visitation ministry. When I arrived at church, I saw that my friend was there too. We decided to team up and go calling together. Snow was beginning to fall, so we decided to take a call not far from the church. We had enough time to make the call and return home before the weather got too bad. In Michigan, our weather could change at a moment's notice. As we left the church, we noticed the snow was coming down a little faster and debated whether we would have enough time to make the call. After deciding that we did, we drove off to find the house. The snow blew even more, making it harder to find the address. Time was going fast! Then it started to sleet, and the streets were beginning to freeze over. What should have been a ten-minute trip turned into an hour, but we finally found the house.

We reached the home's front door and knocked, but there was no answer. We couldn't believe it, after all we had gone through to get there! We were about to leave when someone came to the door. He was a young man in his twenties and was drunk. Nothing seemed to be going right that night! We introduced ourselves and explained why we were there, that his mother had visited our church and we were making a call on her. He said his mother had visited our church but wasn't home. She had left before it started snowing to visit her sister. He also stated he had no interest in church.

We both felt there was a reason for us being there. We gave him a tract, explained it, and asked him if he would promise to read it. He sobered up quickly and promised he would. Shaking our hands and thanking us, he was grateful and highly impressed that we were concerned about his soul and would make a trip out in this weather to visit his mother.

While driving home, as I thought about what took place that night, I realized we had just experienced the love of Jesus Christ for one lost soul! "What man of you, having an hundred sheep, if he lost one of them, doth not leave the ninety and nine in the wilderness, and go after that which is lost, until he find it?" Luke 15:4

Appointment with God

Like many Christians, finding time to read my Bible daily can be a struggle. When we need to go to the doctor, we make an appointment, and the receptionist will give us an option for what time would be best for us. If we have a meeting to attend, we make time to work it into our schedule. Whether it's a doctor's appointment, a ball game, a school function, entertainment, a church activity, or something we like to do, somehow, we find time to fit it into our schedule. Still, we don't do the same thing for God's Word. It is our road map in life! We live in a very busy time! How will we know how to live if we neglect God's Word? "Study to shew thyself approved unto God, a workman that needeth not to be ashamed, rightly dividing the word of truth." Timothy 2:15

I found myself pondering this situation and then came up with a solution. I decided to make a daily appointment with God to read His Word and spend time with Him. I would use a tablet to write down my appointment with Him, also telling God what time I would meet with Him. Doing this gave seriousness to my commitment. Would I want to break my word with God? I would also resist the temptation to read the Bible before my appointment, as it would lessen my commitment to Him. I now find myself keeping tabs on the time; I am concerned about keeping my appointment! I also decided how long I read was unimportant; there wasn't a stopwatch in Heaven timing me! I didn't want it to be a duty but a special time with my Heavenly Father! After all, God keeps His appointments with us.

    Jesus Christ kept His appointment to go to the cross to die for our sins. God keeps every appointment in His Word; He is never late and will always continue to be on time! I realize we will have cancellations due to sickness and situations disrupting our days. God understands these things. The important thing is to get started by making a daily appointment, written down, to meet with God. The clock is ticking - it's time to make an appointment!

Backward and Forward

I have fallen many times through the years due to having a disease called Primary Lateral Sclerosis (PLS). I must say that 99% of the time, I fall backward when I fall. My body knows when it goes off balance to fall backward. Our Christian walk is the same way. When we are in a backsliding state, we regress backward in our walk with the Lord. Our mind and spirit move contrary to what is normal. When we walk in obedience to the Lord, we advance forward, moving onward in our walk.

Each time I fell, I was not given a warning signal that something was about to occur. I would fall! At times, I would be hurt somehow, and at other times, I would be unhurt. The Christian walk is different because God does give us warning signals that we are moving in the wrong direction. Have you ever tried to walk or run backward? It's contrary to normal; eventually, we'll stumble, lose our balance, and fall! The Christian walk is the same way. God gives us warning signals through His Word and the conviction of The Holy Spirit that we are going backward, and if we continue moving contrary to what is normal, we will lose our balance and get off course in our walk with the Lord.

This is why it's so important to read God's Word and go to a church that preaches the Word of God. If we are not warned about sin and don't allow The Holy Spirit to move us in the right direction, we deceive ourselves.

Ask yourself these questions…Am I moving backward or forward in my Christian walk? Are you listening to God's warning signals when The Holy Spirit convicts you that you are going in reverse, contrary to what is normal according to His Word?

Let our thoughts and actions move forward as we follow God's leading through His Word. "And thine ears shall hear a word behind thee, saying, this is the way, walk ye in it, when ye turn to the right hand, and when ye turn to the left." Isaiah 30:20

Balance

Have you ever watched a tight-rope walker as they make their way across a wire cord strung high in the air? I remember watching a tightrope walker on live T.V., slowly crossing a wire cord between two high-rise buildings. Sometimes, I would hold my breath or gasp when he would go slightly off balance. He had a long pole held horizontally to keep his balance. A sound of relief would come from those watching below as he regained his balance. There was no net below to catch him if he fell. One wrong step or gust of wind could throw him off balance! Balance was the key to his victory!

Have you ever felt like your life has become a balancing act as you try to make all your activities fit into your day? There is a saying from long ago that says, "The busier I get, the behind I get!" We go through our days like we're on a tightrope, trying to balance our lives to fit everything in. And just like the tight-rope walker, we also need balance to achieve victory.

Some Christians are content to stay a little off balance, allowing them to do what they want. Having lost their fear and reverence for God and His Word, they can be disobedient in areas that give them more time for the pleasures of life. They are willing to stay a little off balance for desires, not realizing there is a price to pay somewhere along the way. God will allow trials to come our way to help us to get into the right balance. Then, we realize how important it is to obey God's Word.

You may be saying, "That's easier said than done. Life is not that perfect!" You're right; we will never achieve perfection in this life but only in Heaven. That tight-rope walker didn't get that way overnight but with years of discipline and practice. And that's the key to our victory, discipline and practice! If we are weak-willed, it will be harder for us to discipline ourselves. And if we are inclined to a disciplined life, we must direct that toward God. Either way, it will take practice and discipline to direct our thoughts toward God and obedience to His Word. Just as the tight-rope walker fell many times before he could stay balanced on the wire cord, he raised the wire higher and higher as his confidence grew. As we learn to discipline ourselves and grow in confidence in God and His Word, it will take us to higher levels of faith.

When we start out our day by reading God's Word and praying, things seem to fall into place. We have more tranquility in our lives. And as we look to God for "His" direction and depend on "His" strength, our Heavenly Father will stand with us, guiding, directing, and helping us to stay in the right spiritual balance.

"Fear thou not; for I am with thee: be not dismayed; for I am thy God: I will strengthen thee; yea, I will help thee; yes, I will uphold thee with the right hand of my righteousness." Isaiah 41:10

Child Evangelism

The Child Evangelism Association had classes at the Detroit Baptist College to train women from all the different counties, and hundreds of schools were involved. Once a week, women would go into the local schools and teach lessons using flannel graphs and telling the life of Christ. It was in 1970 when one of my friends heard about it and asked if I would be interested in going to see what it was all about, and I said, "yes!" We asked a few more ladies to go, and five of us went. When they opened the session, we heard different testimonies and how God blessed the different schools, bringing hundreds of children to salvation! Then, someone got up and taught the memory verse using a flannel graph. She taught the women there as if we were children; by the time she was done, we all knew the verse! I knew then that I wanted to teach the memory verse!

Mrs. Keys, an elderly lady and the director of the Child Evangelism meetings, taught the flannel graph story. She had been doing this for twenty-five years, and we were spellbound. I had never seen anything like it before. Her hands gracefully and quickly moved the pieces of flannel graph telling the life of Christ. Using different colored lights to highlight the figures, she brought life to the characters just by her expression and the sound of her voice. We knew this was a woman who walked close to the Lord! Each week when she taught the lesson, there was always quietness throughout the auditorium, for she was a "storyteller!" Knowing we were new, some ladies there said, "wait until you hear her teach the Easter story!" We were hooked, and later that year, we did hear her tell the Easter story. Fifty-three years later, I can still see her teaching that story; they were right, it was heart-moving! Mrs. Keys died many years ago, leaving her imprint on the countless lives that crossed her path.

After the Child Evangelism class, my friend went to the local school to get permission to use the program in their elementary school. They were glad to have us come in after school to teach the children. We went to the school the following week and passed out flyers to announce the after-school program. Then we met at my friend's home to decide who would do the different jobs. We got the materials we needed at the meetings: pamphlets, tracts, and the flannel graph. It was time-consuming because we had to color each background with special-colored pencils and cut out all the figures. I had a stamp printing kit that I used to put the memory verse I would teach on a poster board. It was something that we all loved doing.

We were surprised to see how many children came to the first class. Sometimes, as many as twenty or more were in our classes, and many came to salvation! We were in the school for two years. Now, fifty-three years later, times have changed. No longer can you even mention the name of God in our schools. The doors have been closed to the Gospel, but God's Word is still alive and active, spreading the good news that Jesus Christ saves throughout the world! To us who remember the days when we could teach and share the Gospel freely in our schools, it saddens our hearts. I must remind myself that we are in the end times, and God is still in control. Nothing is happening without His permission. I am thankful I was allowed to participate in Child Evangelism and bring the good news to the children that Jesus Christ saves! We will never know how many of those children became missionaries and pastors.

Comfort from God

I was meditating on the comfort of God and thought to myself, how does He comfort us? Comfort is to soothe distress or sorrow, console, help, aid, support, and relieve grief (taken from a dictionary). The word comfort takes in many attributes. How can we apply these attributes to God when we find ourselves in need of comfort? To soothe is to make calm or to have a soothing effect. When I think of comfort, I think of this Psalm, "He maketh me to lie down in green pastures: he leadeth me beside the still waters." Psalm 23:2

I have found in the past that when going through a stressful time, God will bring me to a place of rest. He brings calmness to my spirit, gives rest to my body and mind, and allows me to recuperate, strengthening me to endure a trial that I may be going through. I have often called out to the Lord in my distress, and He has come to my aid in His perfect timing. It may not have been in my timing, but when He knew I was ready to receive it. We take comfort in knowing that when we cry out to God, He hears us and will come to our defense. "In my distress I called upon the Lord, and cried unto my God: he heard my voice out of his temple, and my cry came before him, even into his ears." Psalm 18:6

I remember in 1973 when my father was lying in the hospital and dying from cancer. I was so worn out from my own personal trial that was causing much stress and the grief I felt over my father's pending death that I almost didn't go to the hospital one night. Knowing that my father was in a coma, he wouldn't have known whether I was there. I said to myself, he is my father, and no matter what, even though he wasn't awake, I'm going to the hospital! No sooner had I made that statement, my mind returned to the Seminar my husband and I had attended a few years earlier. I remembered the teaching on singing praises to the Lord when we are by ourselves and how it would uplift us. God spoke to my heart and asked if I could do that as I drove to the hospital. My response was, yes, I could! I sang praises to the Lord from my home to the hospital. I made up the melody as I went along, adding my words of praise.

When I arrived at the hospital, I felt refreshed and calm. Singing praises to the Lord lifted my spirit! "It is a good thing to give thanks unto the Lord, and to sing praises unto thy name, O most High: to show forth thy loving kindness in the morning, and thy faithfulness every night." Psalms 92:1-2. When I arrived at the hospital, my spirit was uplifted, and I was no longer tired and stressed. My mother was with my father when I walked into his room. There he was, sitting up in bed and alert! I stayed for a while, then kissed him and told him I loved him. He said he loved me, too. I left, and three hours later, he died. I was so glad that

God encouraged me to go to the hospital that night and challenged me to sing praises along the way.

God strengthened me in my sorrow and in my trial. God had brought great comfort to my heart. If I had not listened to His still, small voice in my spirit urging me to go, I would have missed a blessing and closure. God has comforted me so many times through His Word, and through the prompting of His Holy Spirit, I found help, aid, and relief from grief. One of my favorite Christian writers is Charles Spurgeon. After my father died, I was reading one of Spurgeon's sermons. God led me to the words of encouragement in his sermon. When I finished reading it, my spirit was lifted, and I rejoiced! God is always there in our hearts, comforting and encouraging when needed. He is the God of all comfort!

"Blessed be God, even the father of our Lord Jesus Christ, the father of mercies, and the God of all comfort."
2 Corinthians 1:3

Commune with Your Heart

"Stand in awe and sin not: commune with your own heart upon your bed, and be still." Psalm 4:4. As I thought about this verse, different words stood out for me.

To stand in awe is to reverence God and acknowledge who He is. I thought about His deity, sovereignty, and His love for me.

We are asked to sin not. Let us have a pureness of heart as we approach God with prayer and awe. We must allow God the Holy Spirit to search our hearts and see if there is any unconfessed sin in our lives. Then, commune with your "own" heart. Did you hear that? Don't worry about someone else's heart other than your own as we approach The Throne of Grace. As we learn to commune with our hearts, God will bring sin to light, and then we are to confess our sin and contemplate what we will ask of Him. We can be concerned about someone's "heart" and their walk with God and pray for them only after our own "heart" is right with Christ our Lord.

Next, be still. Learning to be still is not one of our attributes because of the busyness of our minds. I have a hard time with this because my mind darts off in different directions, and as I get older, I find it's harder to settle down and stay focused. We must learn to push out the worries, fears, tiredness, and any thought that weighs us down. We do this at the very beginning of prayer. As we concentrate and focus on His Attributes, God will reveal unconfessed sin in our lives as we learn to be still. "Thy entrance of thy words giveth light; it giveth understanding unto the simple." Psalm 119:130

Comparing

One thing a Christian should never do
   is to compare ourselves to another

which Satan does use to discourage us
   measuring with Christian brothers.

All have gifts and talents
   with some less and others more.

Our Heavenly Father gives them
   to honor and glorify our Lord.

So be grateful for all you've been given
   and be content with who you are.

Expectations

It was 1966 when I became a Christian, accepting Jesus Christ as my personal Savior, and in 1970, I committed my life to God, asking Him to use me for His Glory. I told God that I was expecting great things from Him. I didn't know what great things specifically, but I had great expectations. I felt confident that God would give me His very best.

Confidence in God was a bold step, but in my mind, it was the only step to take. There is no backing out once we give our lives to God because He is in control! He controls our lives by allowing certain trials for His Glory! In life, we will see Christians with greater trials than our own, and we question how we would endure such a trial. No matter the season, we must trust God, knowing He will receive all the glory.

It was 13 years ago when I had a "big" prayer request for myself. I needed a power wheelchair and a handicapped van. Hebrews 4:16, "Let us therefore come boldly unto the throne of grace, that we may obtain mercy, and find grace to help in time of need." We didn't have the money at that time to purchase either one. My husband, Dean, would often tell me about a man who rode his power wheelchair up and down the streets in our neighborhood and would say, "One day, I'm going to stop that man and talk with him." He wanted to meet him.

There came a day when the man was out riding his wheelchair, and by the time Dean got his wallet and keys for his pickup, the man rode quickly out of sight. Dean decided he was going to find him! He got into his pickup, and off he went on a search. Not long after he left, I heard voices outside in our backyard. He came into the house with a big grin and said, "Come outside and see what is on the driveway." I wasn't sure what to expect, but to my surprise, there was a power wheelchair sitting there! "Wow!" I said, "that was a quick answer to my prayer!" I had prayed my "big" prayer request just the day before.

The man and Dean exchanged our old power mower plus $100.00 for the wheelchair. I needed a power wheelchair, and the man needed a sit-down mower because of his physical condition. Fortunately, we had a sit-down mower that no longer worked and had bought another one. The man had no problem fixing the mower, explaining that he did that for a living before retiring. God had arranged all the events perfectly, knowing how things would unfold to meet my needs and the man's. Dean explained later that the man had a wheelchair in his garage that belonged to his mother-in-law, who had recently passed away. The man said that his mother-in-law would have been pleased that he sold it to me. What a great expectation!

I'm still waiting for a handicapped van. However, I know it will be in God's timing, not mine. "Wait on the Lord: be of good courage, and he shall strengthen thine heart: wait, I say, on the Lord." Psalm 27:14

Set great expectations of God and allow Him to provide the needs of your heart in His perfectly orchestrated way. God wants committed Christians so that He can reveal in us His attributes and demonstrate His abilities to meet our needs, giving God all the glory! "My soul, wait thou only upon God; for my expectation is from him." Psalm 62:5

"But my God shall supply all your need according to his riches in glory by Christ Jesus. Now unto God and our father be glory for ever and ever." Philippians 4:19-20. Amen!

--(I received my handicap van in 2022)

Extreme Makeover

Have you ever thought about having an extreme makeover? I'm not talking about the T.V. programs that renovate your home or having plastic surgery. Did you know you can have a different extreme makeover that won't cost you a penny? I know it's hard to believe because almost everything has a price tag! Did you know someone has already paid the price for you? How can you have this extreme makeover?

Let me introduce you to the person who has paid the price. His name is Jesus Christ. When you accept Jesus Christ as your personal Lord and Savior, He first makes you into a new person.

2 Corinthians 5:18 "Therefore if any man be in Christ, he is a new creature: old things are passed away; behold, all things become new." He also cleanses all the sins from your life and makes you white as snow.

Isaiah 1:18 "Come now, and let us reason together" saith the Lord: "Though your sins be as scarlet, they shall be white as snow; though they be red like crimson, they shall be as wool."

Psalm 103:12 "As far as the East is from the West, so far hath He removed our transgressions from us." Jesus Christ paid the price when He went to the cross and died for our sins, giving us eternal life. When we repent of our sins and receive Him as Lord and Savior, we become born again, starting a new life.

John 3:16 "For God so loved the world that He gave His only begotten son, that whosoever believeth in Him should not perish, but have everlasting life."

After a home is renovated, everyone is invited to see the reconstruction. After plastic surgery, the family is eager to see the results, and the patient is thrilled to display their new look! But what about us Christians - are we excited to display our new life? When you think about it, we have had the ultimate extreme makeover! We are the light of the world! Matthew 5:16 "Let your light so shine before men, that they may see your good works, and glorify your Father which is in Heaven."

Have we forgotten our makeover and lost the excitement about our new life? Matthew 5:14 "Ye are the light of the world. A city that is set on a hill cannot be hid." Are you letting your light shine, still inviting people to see what Jesus Christ has done for you?

We have a new life and an eternal home in Heaven with our Lord Jesus Christ! Plastic surgery may give you a new look, and a reconstructed home may bring comfort in life, but neither holds a candle to the gift that Jesus Christ has given us! John 14:2 "In my father's house are many mansions: if it were not so, I would have told you. I go to prepare a place for you." Are you ready?

Memories

When we think of our past, we have a close acquaintance with it because we know what has already happened. Former things are behind us, and somehow, knowing we cannot change what has already taken place, we are able to put it behind us. But the memories that had a serious effect on us at the time can carry over into the present. We tend to go back and review what has taken place and wonder, if we had made different choices, what our lives would be like now. We have to realize what has been done! It's over. Let it go. We can't change one thing, but we can use our memories to grow and learn from them.

Our experiences, whether good or wrong, can be shared with others to help them avoid the pitfalls they may be heading toward. Our memories can give us compassion toward others when we see them going through what we have already experienced. When we get to Heaven, all memories will be forgotten for they serve no purpose, and all things will become new. But until we get to Heaven, let's put them to rest and awaken those that serve a purpose in this life on earth. I remember hearing Corrie Ten Boom speak at a ladies' conference and the encouragement she gave by sharing her memories of what took place in her life. How her faith sustained her through the sufferings she went through. Our memories are important not only to us but also to others.

We never know when our paths will cross with someone going through a trial we have already experienced and share with them how we overcame it.

God can bring healing in many ways and will bring a memory to the surface in times of need. Romans 8:28 "And we know that God causes all things to work together for good to them who love God, to them who are called according to His purpose."

Flowers

When I walked home from school
I would stop and pick flowers.

They were blue violets that grew in a patch,
then took them home to my mother.

She would take the violets as pleased as could be,
and place them in a glass of water for all to see.

At times I'd pick dandelions with
Bright yellow buds.

My mother was just as pleased with them.
I knew this because of her little hugs!

"Consider the lilies how they grow: they toil not,
they spin not; and yet I say unto you,
that Solomon in all his glory was not arrayed like one of
these." Luke 12:27

Focusing

I can remember the first time when I looked through high-power binoculars. I was in my twenties, and they were my husband's. It was fascinating to see objects that were far off in the distance come in close. I searched from one object to another, drawing them close to get a better glimpse. I also learned that I had to adjust the lens on the binoculars for my eyes to get a clearer image; otherwise, everything would have been a blur.

Sometimes, we may feel like we are in a blur about ourselves and would like to get a better glimpse of what is going on in our lives. God's Word is His binocular that searches out our hearts. His Word can reveal areas in our lives that are not according to His will and may be off in the distance by bringing them into focus, removing the blur, and giving us a clearer image of who we are in Christ. "I the Lord search the heart, I try the reins, even to give every man according to his ways and the fruit of his doings." Jeremiah 17:10

Some are not Christians and may try to distance themselves from God by not acknowledging their sin and repenting. "Can any hide himself in secret places that I shall not see him? Saith the Lord. Do not I fill heaven and earth? Saith the Lord?" Jeremiah 23:24

God seeks the lost by drawing them close, revealing salvation from sin through Jesus Christ our Lord. God is a seeker of hearts! "No man can come to me, except the father which hath sent me draw him: and I will raise him up at the last day." John 6:44

God does not have to adjust anything to get a better glimpse of us, for He is sovereign and all-knowing. "Hast thou not known? Hast thou not heard, that the everlasting God, the Lord, the Creator of the ends of the earth, fainted not, neither is weary? There is no searching of His understanding." Isaiah 40:28. Christians need to adjust the lens of their lives by opening their hearts as they focus on the Word of God, getting a clearer image of who they are in Christ Jesus. Although we may sometimes wander from Him, His focus always stays upon us.

Let us draw near to God as He searches out our hearts, revealing those things that we have put far off in the distance, making known the hidden places of sin that may hinder our walk with the Lord.

"For the ways of man are before the Lord, and he pondereth all his goings." Proverbs 5:21.

His Very Best

I thought about people going through all walks of life with different trials unique to each person. As Christians, God has been preparing us for every trial we go through so that we are not overwhelmed by them. Each trial we go through prepares us for the next one. Knowing that we have God's very best will make us view our trials differently. Each trial's purpose is to strengthen our faith in Him and conform us to Christ's image.

You may ask, how do we know we have God's very best? Because God cannot make a mistake, He is perfect in all His ways. 2 Samuel 22:31 says, "As for God, his way is perfect; the word of the Lord is tried: he is a buckler to all them that trust in him." This is why it's important to learn to trust Him. He knows exactly what we need and how, when, and where. You can rest assured that His ways are best for us.

God brings discipline and blessings into our lives as He watches over and cares for us. Christians watch others as they go through their trials, thinking they could never live like that, but you would be surprised at what you can do if God has been preparing you for that very trial. He will give you strength to endure as you grow in grace. Your faith will strengthen, and you can look back and know you had His very best.

If someone had told me years ago that I would have Primary Lateral Sclerosis and its physical effect on me, I would have been discouraged just thinking about it. Now that I have PLS, I know His grace is sufficient to meet all my needs. All our trials, whether big or small, will stretch our faith as we learn to trust Him. It's not always easy to be stretched. It feels like our lives are being torn apart, and we want to say, "That's enough; I can't take anymore!" If you take something that can be stretched and then let go, it will return to its original form. God knows just how far to stretch us without breaking us. When a trial fulfills God's purpose for our lives, He releases the pull, and we return to our original form, only stronger in the Lord.

"In the day when I cried thou answeredst me, and strengthenedst me with strength in my soul." Psalm 138:3

Imprints in Life

In a few of my devotions, I've talked about different people and how they left their imprint in life. I've also talked about the impression they had left on my life. I thought about movie stars down through the years who had left their footprints or handprints immortalized in a cement walkway outside Grauman's Chinese Theatre in Hollywood, leaving their legacy behind. This imprint formed in cement seemed to give them fame and recognition in life. Sadly, if they did not have Jesus Christ in their lives, their imprints left no meaning other than what the world could offer. An imprint leaves behind a characteristic or a result. Jesus Christ left His imprint in life. We not only saw His character, but we saw the result of His life! As we walk through this life, what imprint are we leaving behind?

How does one leave an imprint in life? By following in the steps of Jesus Christ, being filled with His Holy Spirit, and walking in the Word of God. It's not always easy, and there will be times when we will stumble. But as we focus on God's Word, our steps become secure, leaving an imprint behind - an impression on our life's walk.

I thought about the author, Corrie Ten Boom. The very first Christian book I read was her book called, "The Hiding Place." During World War 2, her Christian family hid Jews and others during the Nazi occupation in a secret room behind a false wall in their home. When discovered, her family was sent to a concentration camp. What an impact her autobiography left on my life as a young Christian! Years later, I had the opportunity to hear her speak at a Women's Retreat. She was in her early seventies at that time. I was looking forward to seeing her in person! I remember watching as she was slowly escorted to the stage. She walked with a bent posture using a cane and was short in stature. She wore a light blue dress, and her white hair twirled in a bun. She sat in a chair and shared what God meant to her life and her walk with Him over many years. Here was a woman who left her imprint in life for others to see. To see such a Spirit-filled person left a tremendous impression on my life!

I thought about walking along a sandy beach, leaving our footprints in the sand. Soon, the tide washes away those footprints. As Christians, our walk should be on the solid rock, which is Jesus Christ, our Lord! To do otherwise, the world will wash away our imprint. Jesus is always a step ahead of us, leaving His imprint in life showing the way in which we should walk. As we follow in His footsteps, we will also leave an impression - our imprint in life! "For even hereunto were ye called: because Christ also suffered for us, leaving us an example, that ye should follow his steps."
I Peter 2:21

Living Life Over

While lying in bed sick with a sinus infection, I was watching "Ann of Green Gables," one of my many favorite movies. I was envious of that time period and wondered if I had lived during that time, what would have been different about me? I wondered if my background had been different, would I have been different too? I wondered if the difficulties I faced in life would have changed. My thoughts turned to God and His Word. God knew me before I was born. "For thou hast possessed my reins: thou hast covered me in my mother's womb." Psalm 139:14. My mother was already chosen for me. The time of my birth was preordained. "A time to be born." Ecclesiastes 3:2a.

I had no control over who my parents would be or where I would live. My personality, features, and my talents were all preordained before I was born. God had a definite pattern for my life. To say I wish I was born to different parents or in a different time period is to say that God made a mistake. God, perfect in all His ways, cannot make a mistake. "He is the rock. His work is perfect: for all his ways are judgment: a God of truth and without iniquity, just and right is he." Deuteronomy 32:4

In history, each generation has had its own troubles and woes. If we could go back and live life over again, we would find nothing new under the sun. Living in a different time period would not have made you a better person. We would still experience the stresses of life, trials, and disease. "The things that hath been, it is that which shall be; and that which is done is that which shall be done: and there is no new thing under the sun." Ecclesiastes 1:9.

We like to dream of what we could be, and there is nothing wrong with this, for it gives us a goal to strive for. To be discontent with who we are because we are disappointed in ourselves does not mean we would be any different if we could live life over again. Of course, if we could go back and correct the mistakes that we made during our lives, we would be different, but God has not given us that option. We must learn to be content with who we are. If there are areas in our lives that make us unhappy, then by all means, by the grace of God, change what you can. We cannot turn back the clock of time nor feel that, somehow, we missed out on life. If you feel like your life is in a mess and are discontent, remember God's love and how He cares and watches over you.

I can remember my mother teaching me how to do embroidery when I was a young girl. My first piece had butterflies and flowers on it. By placing each stitch onto the pattern and following my mother's instructions, the back side was a total mess when I was finished, with threads going every which way! When I compared it to my mother's embroidery, the back of her piece was just as neat as the front. My mother learned over the years of embroidery how to place her stitches so that the back side was just as neat as the front side. Our lives work on the same principle. We may feel that we are a mess, but as we turn our lives over to the Lord, we learn that with each step of obedience we take, we become more skillful as we learn to follow God's instructions…His pattern for our lives.

We must learn to be content with who we are as God weaves us into His chosen pattern. Sometimes, we will mess up our lives and wish we could live life over. We can learn from those mistakes by following God's Word and ensuring that our life steps are in the right pattern according to His instructions. As we acquire wisdom, our lives inside and out will be straight and in the same direction as we follow the Lord.

Measures

Did you know that God used measures in His creation? When creating the earth, God measured the span of the earth and heavens. "Who hath measured the waters in the hollow of his hand, and meted out heaven with a span, comprehended the dust of the earth in a measure, and weighed the mountains in scales, and the hills in a balance?" Isaiah 40:12

Everything that God created was measured. The only one who cannot be measured is God. He is immeasurable. "Before the mountains were brought forth, or ever thou hadst formed the earth and the world, even from everlasting to everlasting, thou art God." Psalm 90:2

God has given people a measure of faith that will allow them to receive Jesus Christ as Savior, leading to salvation so that they are without excuse. How we use our measure of faith will be our choice. "For I say, through the grace given unto me, to every man among you, not to think more highly than he ought to think, but to think soberly, according as God hath dealt to every man the measure of faith." Romans 12:3

No matter what we experience, His grace will be sufficient for as much as is needed. "And God is able to make all grace abound toward you; that ye, always having all sufficiency in all things, may abound to every good work." 2 Corinthians 9:8

Our days on Earth have also been measured. God has given mankind a measure of time on this earth. "Lord, make me to know my end, and the measure of my days, what it is; that I may know how frail I am." Psalm 39:4

When God corrects us, it is done in measure. He will allow trials that are measured to enter our lives to teach us and conform us to the image of Christ. His correction is in accordance with His Word, our Bible, which gives us a standard to live by. Let us use our measures in life wisely, allowing them to mature us in the ways of God. "So teach us to number our days, that we may apply our hearts unto wisdom." Psalm 90:12

Worry

I asked myself a question, "Why do we worry?" What is it that we are trying to achieve? We usually worry about things that are out of our control, something we can't change. It reminds me of a mouse going around and around in a cage on a treadmill and getting nowhere! We think that if we keep going over the problem, "the treadmill in our mind," we can change the problem.

Worry is how we attach ourselves to a problem that gives a sense of control. It shows our prideful flesh! Worry can also be a habit that we have developed over the years. It's hard to break a habit, for once sin gains a stronghold, we find ourselves in warfare. The flesh wants control, and God is asking us to trust Him.

God's Word tells us not to worry nor to be anxious. He also gave us a guideline on how to think. "Finally, brethren, whatsoever things are true, whatsoever things are honest, whatsoever things are just, whatsoever things are pure, whatsoever things are lovely, whatsoever thing is of a good report; if there be any virtue, and if there be any praise, think on these things." Philippians 4:8

How rewarding it would be to give our problems to God, to wait upon Him with prayer and supplication. Only He can bring about the change we seek. Think of all the stress you would save yourself by not worrying! With anticipation, we look forward to the glory He would receive from yielding our lives to Him. Learn to wait upon the Lord Jesus Christ and rest in His sovereignty. The more we learn about God, the easier it will be to trust His Word.

Before you get on the treadmill of worry, stop and think about what God has said by focusing on His Word rather than on yourself. Let go of worry and allow Him to carry your burden. Matthew 11:29-30 "Take my yoke upon you, and learn of me; for I am meek and lowly in heart: and ye shall find rest unto your souls. For my yoke is easy, and my burden is light."

Putty

Have you ever heard someone say, "Ah, they were putty in my hands," meaning they could persuade or maneuver the person into doing what they wanted? When working with putty, you have to press it to conform to your desired mold. Have you ever felt like putty in someone's hands? Some people are very skilled when dealing with others' feelings. They know how to manipulate and use persuasion to get what they want; if they were up-front with them, they might not get their way.

My husband, Dean, and I took a course at the Detroit Bible College many years ago. After class one night, I shared a little with our professor about some things I had been experiencing and asked him a question. His answer was, "God gave us a brain, and He expects us to use it." I knew that I needed no further explanation. I thought about Satan and how we can become putty in his hands. He can maneuver and use persuasion through our thoughts, and we are unaware of his deception.

If we are going to be putty in someone's hands, then let it be God's. He would not manipulate but persuade us through His love and Word. "But now, O Lord, thou art our father; we are the clay, and thou our potter; and we all are the work of thy hand." Isaiah 64:8

As we go through different trials, we may feel squeezed and pressed on all sides, just like putty. Think of each squeeze as a hug from God and each pressing as a reminder that He is still working in your life. Many years ago, I gave permission to God to do whatever He deemed necessary in my life that would bring honor and glory unto Him. I don't know why I needed to say this to God as if He needed my permission. Many times down through the years, when life got tough, He has reminded me of my permission. Would I do the same thing knowing what I know now? The answer is "yes." Through the years, I have renewed this permission as a reminder that my trials work for my good. Since my commitment to God, I've had many hugs and reminders letting me know He is still working in my life, bringing honor and glory unto Him.

"That the trial of your faith, being much more precious than of gold that perisheth, though it be tried with fire, might be found unto praise and honour and glory at the appearing of Jesus Christ." 1 Peter 1:7

Ready, Set, Go

I can remember, as a child, running races with the neighborhood kids. We would use a large stick or whatever we could find to mark off the finish line. Someone would stand at the sideline and shout, "ready, set, go!" We would run like the dickens trying to win the race! To get ready was to find our place in line. "Set" was to stand in position, and of course, "go" was the start of the race. Let's parallel this with the Christian life.

Ready…prepared in mind. Be willing to find your place in life. We have all been given different spiritual gifts at the start of our salvation and God-given talents at birth. What are yours? Find out where your talent lies and what spiritual gifts you have. Then, find your place in life and serve God wholeheartedly.

Set…fixed in your position. Set your mind to the goal ahead. Know in which direction God wants you to move. In the Bible, you will find directions for your life and what your goals should be.

Go…release your hold on life by stepping out in faith and trusting God to help you run the race to the finish line.

When we become Christians, receiving Jesus Christ as our personal Savior upon repentance, we have entered a race. "Wherefore seeing we also are compassed about with so great a cloud of witnesses, let us lay aside every weight, and the sin which doth easily beset us, and let us run with patience the race that is set before us." Hebrews 12:1

We must be prepared to run this race to the finish line using our talents and spiritual gifts. Everyone has at least one of the following gifts: wisdom, faith, discerning spirit, helping, teaching, exhortation, giving, showing of mercy, evangelism, and pastor-teacher. As we exercise our spiritual gifts and talents, we bring honor and glory unto our Lord Jesus Christ.

Know your position in Jesus Christ. To know our position is to know who we are in Christ. We are loved and have been adopted into God's family. We have obtained an inheritance and are indwelled and empowered by God the Holy Spirit. God has given us every qualification needed to run our race.

We are to go in God's power and might, witnessing to a lost world. "Go ye therefore, and teach all nations, baptizing them in the name of the Father, and of the Son, and of the Holy Ghost, teaching them to observe all things whatsoever I have commanded you; and lo, I am with you alway, even unto the end of the world." Matthew 28:19-20. As we use our spiritual gifts and talents, reaching out to others, we are ready to run our race with all that God has given us. Christians! Ready, Set, Go!

Shining Through

    At our church in Michigan, in a Sunday morning service, our pastor announced we would have a special guest speaker. This speaker would share the Word of God, sing, and play the organ for us the following Sunday morning. He also said that the guest speaker would be different from us but did not explain what the difference would be.

    The following Sunday morning, as the sanctuary began filling up, many looked forward to hearing this man speak. We also wondered why he would be different from us. After our pastor introduced him, he was pushed out in a wheelchair. Our pastor was right. He was different from us. He didn't have any arms or legs! He had stumps for arms and legs. I know most of us felt uncomfortable not knowing what to expect. I think we were also feeling uncomfortable for him.

    After being introduced, he gave his testimony and shared how God had worked in his life. His testimony was a blessing to all of us! Then he introduced his family. An attractive young woman came walking out with their two small daughters. I had to admit I was surprised to see he was married. He asked his wife to come and share what God had laid on her heart. She gave her testimony, how they met, and the love God had placed in her heart for her husband.

An organ was rolled out that was made especially for him. The keyboard was made with wider keys to fit his limbs. He began to play and sing, and sing and play, he did! He was great! He had a wonderful voice! I think we were all surprised! What seemed impossible became possible! For the next hour, he sang and shared the Word of God with us, and soon, his physical appearance didn't seem to matter anymore. He was a man of God! The love of God was shining through him and reaching into our hearts.

God taught all of us a very important lesson that morning. We may be limited in many ways, but God is never limited! This man had accepted his limitations and trusted God with what he had, and God truly blessed him! "But Jesus beheld them, and said unto them. With men this is impossible: but with God all things are possible." Mark 10:27

Suffering

It was in 2016 when I went to the Emory ALS Clinic for my yearly checkup. It was an all-day affair waiting for each specialist to come to my room—questions to answer, muscles tested for strength, pulmonary check-up, and sometimes a memory test. I usually knew all the people who came to my room, but this day, I had a new specialist that I had never seen before. A young neurologist came in and introduced himself. Shaking hands, he pulled up a chair and sat before me. He held my hand, pulled my arm toward my leg, and laid my hand next to my knee. He continued to hold my hand and then started to stare at my arm. This was a new test for me. He was so intense, staring at my arm. I kept quiet, and my husband too. A few minutes went by while he stared at my arm. He never spoke a word. Finally, my curiosity got the best of me, and I had to ask him what he was looking for. He said he was looking for fluctuations on my arm for symptoms of ALS. I asked him if he saw any, and he said no. Everything looked good. I thought back to 2001 when I was diagnosed with Primary Lateral Sclerosis and asked if I had ever heard of ALS. At that time, I could feel a chill go through me. But this time, I took it in stride.

I never gave ALS much thought until 2016, when I was tested for it. Even though I was told many years ago, that PLS could evolve into ALS. I don't know what the future will hold for me, but whatever it is, I know God is in control and will supply my needs as I continue in life.

Whatever comes to us that is beyond our control, Jesus Christ knows our suffering. Our thought process to remain positive can be challenging as we look to God to sustain us through the unsuspected changes that suffering can bring into our lives. We may endure deep pain and anguish that alters our way of living. However, we must always depend on God's Word, as every promise given in His Word is ours to receive. It is good to read His promises to reassure us that He will never leave us on our own, and most assuredly, He will keep His promises.

When my heart feels unsettled, I go to the book of Psalms, where I find comfort and reassurance in times of need. Psalm 31:24 "Be of good courage, and he shall strengthen your heart, all ye that hope in the Lord." Be brave of heart and wait for something to happen as we hope in the Lord. He will give us the inner strength to endure our suffering. As we look to Jesus Christ in times of suffering, let us lean on Him, not our own understanding. Our suffering should draw us closer to God if we allow it. There is a purpose behind suffering that only God can bring about as we learn to depend on Him and rest in His sovereignty. Proverbs 3:5-6 "Trust in the Lord with all thine heart; and lean not unto thine own understanding. In all thy ways acknowledge him, and he shall direct your paths."

The Conductor

Have you ever been to a symphony and watched the conductor as he directed the instrumentalist in a musical selection? As the musicians play their instruments following the written score before them, they watch the conductor guide them through the composition. The conductor, at times, is up on his toes as he waves his baton to the music and cues the musicians when to start with their instruments. It's his job to keep everyone in rhythm.

God has orchestrated all things and conducts everything according to His perfect will. As Christians, think of yourselves as His instruments as He directs, guides, and fine-tunes us according to His will. God's Words are our notes in life that keep us in rhythm as He directs our paths. If we are offbeat, He has a way of getting our attention as He gently uses His baton to get us back into the right rhythm of life. As His instruments, it's important to keep our eyes on His notes. If we get distracted and do not follow His written score, we soon find ourselves off-beat, losing our place in rhythm.

Each note in life brings us closer to the completion of our composition. If we go by our own beat and ignore our conductor, "following our own rhythm in life," we find our lives ending with no melody to be heard. We all have heard music when someone plays or sings off-key; we grimace and cringe at the sound, knowing it does not fit into the music. Like a piano tuner, when playing a key, they can hear if it's off-tune and adjust the strings to refine the tone. When we read God's Word, do we hear if we are out of tune in our walk with The Lord and adjust our ways?

What about your composition in life, and how do you want to finish it? Do you want to follow our Conductor's notes and stay in rhythm as He guides you through life?

What will your life melody be? Will it have a lasting effect on those who have heard it? When your melody is in tune with The Lord, bringing a beautiful harmonious sound, others will hear with rejoicing and praising The Lord!

"Speaking to yourselves in psalms and hymns and spiritual songs, singing and making melody in your heart to the Lord." Ephesians 5:19

The Last Rose

My daughter and her husband gave me a rose bush for Mother's Day one year. My husband planted it in direct line with my recliner lift chair so I could easily see the rose bush through the patio window in our backyard. I watched it every day and saw the roses grow larger and fuller with the most vibrant and bright shade of red.

When fall arrived, it was at the end of October when we had our first frost. I wondered if the roses would survive, and they did. After the second frost, I thought for sure I would find them lying on the ground and was surprised to see they were still in the bush! After the third frost, they fell to the ground and withered away. While looking at the fallen roses on the ground, I saw a rose hanging close to the bottom of the bush. It was the only rose left in the bush. The leaves and roses that were up above covered and shielded the rose from the frost. The last rose stayed in the bush for another two weeks before falling to the ground.

I thought to myself, Christians are like that red rose; we can be strong in the Lord as He shelters us from the storms of life. We have a Heavenly Father who watches over us and shields us as we go through the trials and tribulations of life. Jesus Christ will never leave nor forsake us as we trust Him; we can endure all seasons.

"He shall cover thee with his feathers, and under his wings shall thou trust: his truth shall be thy shield and buckler." Psalms 91:4

The Luncheon

In 2019, I entered my 24th year with Primary Lateral Sclerosis, and how fast the years have flown by. Little by little each year I would lose a certain amount of strength in my voluntary muscles. It was so gradual it really didn't have a major effect on me until later years. I was able to walk on my own, go up and down steps with ease, and still drive. My speech was the first to be affected but that was gradual too.

I was eight years into my disease when I received an email from a woman whose spouse had PLS and was planning a luncheon for PLS patients in Georgia. She wanted to meet at a restaurant and wanted to know if I could attend. Of course, I wanted to go and said yes. She was in my nationwide PLS group online and had access to my email address. At that time, I was using a walker, as my legs were getting weak. She told me that five patients were coming. I then found out that there were only five PLS patients in the state of Georgia, which included myself. On the day of the luncheon, her husband decided he was too weak to come and decided to stay home. She had invited a physical therapist who was very knowledgeable about PLS to join us and give a lecture.

She chose a restaurant that would be best for all of us so that we wouldn't have to travel long. The goal was for us to have to travel no more than two hours to the restaurant and luckily it only took my husband and me one hour. As soon as we arrived at the restaurant, I was feeling nervous and excited at the same time. I had never met other patients with PLS. Going into the restaurant, I saw one patient in a wheelchair and one with a walker.

    My husband and I sat across a young man that looked to be in his late thirties. He was with a young lady who was a friend of his. He let out a grunt from deep within his chest, which surprised me! I didn't realize he was a PLS patient. His friend announced to others that he could not talk at all and when he had something to say he would let out a grunt to get our attention. He had a computer, but different from my Dynawrite, and it would speak for him as he typed his words. I asked him how long he had PLS, and he typed in five years. Using his computer, he introduced himself and where he was from. He shared about losing his voice and the impact it had on him, and typed, "He would give anything to hear the sound of his voice again." I understood him, a grunt was not the sound he wanted to hear. It was the actual sound of his voice, something so many take for granted, that he longed to hear.

    We were asked to share about our lives. Of course, me and the young man couldn't share, so my husband spoke on my behalf and the young man's friend spoke for him. My husband shared our Christian faith and how God has sustained us over the years. The woman in the wheelchair also shared about her faith and having PLS.

The five of us would go on different paths with our PLS, some would progress faster while others, a slow progression. It was important for me not to focus on wheelchairs, losing my voice, or creating a negative outlook for myself. I had already been told by my neurologist what to expect that may come my way. Being a Christian and knowing God would provide all my needs, I would not dwell on the "what ifs."

I thought of the man that was in one of my devotions called, "Being a Christian," who lost the use of his hands from PLS and how God used his voice to share about his PLS and the Gospel in churches throughout Georgia. I prayed that one day this young man sitting across from me would allow God to use him in a special way. His friend had shared that he was a Christian too.

There are times when we feel like we are caught up in a whirlwind with different emotions being tossed about and swept off our feet with unexpected situations and a feeling of desperation. We are looking for answers and a way out. When our focus is on The Lord Jesus Christ, only He can calm the whirlwinds we find ourselves in, and we are trusting that He is in control. Mark 4:39, "And he arose, and rebuked the wind, and said unto the sea, Peace be still. And the wind ceased, and there was a great calm." As we choose to trust God, eventually the whirling winds will begin to calm down and dispel, and we find ourselves at peace with the trial that God allowed to touch our lives.

My mind went back sixteen years ago to the PLS luncheon and the young man that lost his voice from this disease. I remember seeing the desperate look in his eyes and the sadness. His emotions were in a whirlwind knowing that the sound of his voice would never be heard again. I'm sure Christians who knew this young man were praying for him. I trust that the whirlwind he felt he was in calmed down and gradually went away as he learned to trust God and was at peace. When something overwhelming comes our way, remember to focus on God and His promises and not get caught up in a whirlwind.

"Therefore I take pleasure in infirmities, in reproaches, in necessities, in persecutions, in distresses for Christ's sake: for when I am weak, then am I strong."
2 Corinthians 12:10

Trust

I'm in my twenty-first year with my disease, Primary Lateral Sclerosis. In the early stage of my disease, which started in 1996, I could do activities that I can no longer do. It is now 2017. Early on with my PLS, it really wasn't that bad, as I could still walk, drive, and do the same activities as I had done before. The only symptom I had was related to my speech. It was hard to pronounce words. Because of my speech, in time, I had to quit working. My last three jobs were in sales, and because I struggled when speaking with customers and answering the phone, I had to retire.

Now, twenty-one years later, it's a different story. There are so many things that I cannot do, simple things like putting on a coat and so many other little things that I used to take for granted like walking, running, going up and down steps, vacuuming, cooking, etc. But, somehow, you adjust to your circumstances and, over time, develop techniques to take up the slack in doing tasks. The mind can be very creative when trying to solve a difficult task. I learned to brace myself against a table or counter for balance when I had to use my hands or whatever else was handy at the time to keep from falling. I have used a walker for fifteen years now and use it for carrying items on the seat, using the handles as a brace, too. Of course, my computer has been a blessing. It's given me the opportunity to write and to communicate with friends on Facebook and email.

It's not significant for me to share all my symptoms with people. What is important, however, is how I respond to God and how I represent Him regarding my disease. My attitude toward my disease expresses my trust in The Lord. It can encourage other believers to trust in God's promises, knowing that He will be with us to the very end.

Life is full of choices; we can choose to be unhappy over our circumstances, demonstrating untrust toward God, or we can believe when we go through a trial that The Lord has a plan to increase our faith in Him and strengthen us within our spirit. What will your choice be? Will you choose to bring honor and glory unto God? Psalms 37:5 "Commit thy way unto the Lord; trust also in him; and he shall bring it to pass."

– It is now the year 2023.

Weighing Our Words

I can remember as a child hearing these words, "Think before you speak." We should learn to weigh our words. Just think, if everyone would practice this saying, what a difference it would make in people's lives! Demeaning remarks would not shatter our confidence, and our self-esteem would be higher. With encouraging words, we could face new challenges without fear and be willing to take more risks. We would set more goals for ourselves and receive criticism and advice without being offended, becoming positive people!

We must also learn to weigh our words against our own selves. Belittling ourselves is self-destructive. Putting ourselves down, comparing and measuring ourselves to others, and dwelling on the negative can lead to self-pity. We can blame others for our failures, but there comes a time when we must grow up and accept responsibility for our own actions. Your personality, features, parents, environment, and abilities were all given by God to bring about His plan for your life, first to bring you to a saving knowledge of Jesus Christ, then to mold and make you into His image. Isaiah 64:8 "But now, O Lord, thou art our father; we are the clay, and thou our potter; and we are the work of thy hand."

If we must compare ourselves, compare ourselves against The Word of God, not what others may think of us.

There will always be people who are more attractive, smarter, and talented than you are. The problem is that we see ourselves from the inside out, all the junk that has accumulated over the years. But if you're a child of God, He can take that junk and turn it into treasure. We are to shine under the grace of God!

Pressing on means there will be pressure as God molds us into His image. As we learn to weigh our words toward others and ourselves in a positive manner according to the Word of God and walk in His Spirit, we will begin to see ourselves in His light! Matthew 5:16 "Let your light so shine before men, that they may see your good works, and glorify your father which is in heaven."

Now take a deep breath and quit worrying about what you are not but what you can be as you yield your life to God! Philippians 4:8 "Finally, brethren, whatsoever things are true, whatsoever things are honest, whatsoever things are just, whatsoever things are pure, whatsoever things are lovely, whatsoever thing are of a good report; if there be any virtue, and if there be any praise, think on these things." When we put this verse into practice and learn to trust Him, our lives will bring honor and glory unto God!

Yesterday, Today, and Tomorrow

I often said to myself, "if I had a nickel for every time I dropped something, I would be rich!" As my disease, Primary Lateral Sclerosis, has progressed, my hands have become weaker. So far, I have not dropped a glass, and not one of my favorite dishes. Pencils and silverware seemed to be my favorite things to drop! At times, I would get angry and feel frustrated, but then, this thought would come to mind. By dropping things, I would have to bend over and pick the object up. This was not an easy task for me, but just the exercise I needed to keep my limbs from becoming stiff. I thought of a verse in the Bible. "And we know all things work together for good to them that love God, to them who are called according to his purpose." Romans 8:28. Even a simple task such as picking something up off the floor worked for my good!

I'm trying not to focus on the mistakes or failures of yesterday but to learn from them. I know that when I'm feeling down, it's due to focusing on my limitations rather than the unlimited grace of God. As Christians, our achievements and failures are part of God's plan for our lives…even our illnesses!

I can't focus on tomorrow. No one knows what tomorrow will hold other than what my imagination can conjure up. God tells us that tomorrow will take care of itself. That leaves only today to concentrate upon. I have only today to learn to trust God, grow in grace, and claim His promises. We often fail, but that doesn't give us an excuse to give up. God's Word teaches us just the opposite. "For a just man falleth seven times, and riseth up again: but the wicked shall fall into mischief." Proverbs 24:16

When we fall, we rise again, returning to the course of serving our Savior. Yesterday is gone. We must learn from it and go on. Don't waste energy worrying about tomorrow; after all, you might not be here! Only today is left. Seek out God's will for your life and be all you can be. In the end, God will receive the glory and honor as you learn to trust each day to Him. "This is the day the Lord has made; we will rejoice and be glad in it." Psalm 118:24

Comforting Words

Down through the years, I have read Psalms 139 many times. One day, while reading this chapter, two verses that comforted my heart stood out. I was so overwhelmed by these two verses that I would like to share with you what they meant to me.

"How precious also are thy thoughts unto me, O God!" How great is the sum of them! If I should count them, they are more in number than the sand: I am still with thee when I awake." Psalm 139:17-18. I thought about all the beaches, sand dunes, and deserts that would be throughout the world, yet His thoughts toward me were greater than all the grains of sand on earth! I felt a closeness to God that I had never felt before. He continually thinks of me, not only of me but all His children! How infinite are His thoughts! I knew I was on His mind, but the vastness of His thoughts toward me took me to a deeper level of understanding of the depths of His love.

I don't think I will ever fully understand His infiniteness, self-existence, capacity, fullness, and perfection, until I get to Heaven. It is too much for my mind to comprehend. Now, when I find myself in worry, how foolish I feel, doubting that God will meet all my needs. God is endless; limits or boundaries do not bind him. He is the self-existent One, the great I Am! We find comfort in His

Word as we take it to heart and claim all He has for us. A promise from God cannot be taken back because it was spoken in perfection. "Who comforteth us in all our tribulation, that we may be able to comfort them which are in any trouble, by the comfort wherewith we ourselves are comforted of God." 2 Corinthians 1:4

God the Holy Spirit is our comforter. "But when the Comforter is come, whom I will send unto you from the Father, even the Spirit of truth, which proceedeth from the Father, he shall testify of me." John 16:26

He will comfort us through all our tribulation and be our teacher as He reveals God's truth through His Word. He understands us fully, every aspect of our lives before Him, for His thoughts are continually toward us with a father's love.

"Great is the Lord, and of great power: his understanding is infinite." Psalm 147:5

Made in the USA
Columbia, SC
03 December 2024